Pupil's Book 3

Chris Buckton
Anne Sanderson

Series editor: Leonie Bennett

Symbols

PCM A photocopy master is available to support differentiation.

Differentiation symbols.

1 Easy to complete.

2 All pupils complete activity. Activities are supported by a PCM for extra help.

3 More difficult activities.

Author Team: Chris Buckton
Anne Sanderson
Series Editor: Leonie Bennett

Ginn
Linacre House, Jordan Hill, Oxford, OX2 8DP
a division of Reed Educational and Professional Publishing Ltd
www.ginn.co.uk

ISBN 0602 296803

04 03 02 01
10 9 8 7 6 5 4 3

Designed and produced by Gecko Ltd, Bicester, Oxon
Cover design by Gecko Ltd, Bicester, Oxon
Printed in Spain by Edelvives

Contents

STORY IDEAS

Talking to Jamila Gavin

Where do you get your ideas for stories?

'To start with, they come from inside me. A good way of getting going is to make a star chart. You can do a star chart about yourself first. You write ME in the middle and then ask lots of questions round the edges. When you write a story you're always asking questions, like Who? What? Where? Why? When? How?'

How do you make up characters?

'You can use a star chart to ask questions about a character you want to use in a story. I write the name of a character in the middle and then I ask: What's my character doing? How did he get there? Why does he behave like he does? Where is he going? What's going to happen?'

How do you plan the story?

'The beginning of a story sets the scene and explains how the character got there. This is the background. Then something has to happen, like a problem – that's what gets the story going. And then, what happens next? In fairy stories, it might be magic. In real life stories, it might be somebody who helps you out, or you might find something. And then something has to happen at the end to make it all come right.'

What would be your top tip for people writing stories?

'Write about things that really mean something to you.'

WRITING A STORY

Brainstorm

Plan

Draft

Revise

Reading

1. Make your own ME star chart. Answer the questions on **sheet 1**. Make notes in the space provided. Talk about it with a partner.

2. Add some more questions to the chart.

Writing

Use an idea from your star chart to help you plan a story. Use **sheet 2**.

1. Brainstorm ideas for setting, characters and events.

2. Start to plan your story.

- Write all your ideas down.
- Choose the best ideas.
- Start to invent things.

Extended Writing

Use your plan to write a first draft of your story. Try to include all your best ideas.

STORY SETTING

Familiar Places

vivid description

Suddenly, Kate noticed a huge removal van draw up outside Number 82. The house had been empty for ages, and the gardens at the front and back had become quite wild. Some naughty children had discovered a hole in the fence and sneaked through after dark to steal apples, and collect the blackberries which trailed across the over-grown lawn.

It had seemed as though the house would stay empty for ever ... The 'For Sale' notice which had stood in front for ages had fallen down long ago ...

Kate stopped swinging on the gate and walked out on to the pavement. She began to feel excited. Was a new family moving in at last?

From *Kamla and Kate* by Jamila Gavin

make the reader want to read on

Wayne wasn't the only one in his family who liked football. On Saturday mornings Wayne's Dad played for a team called Even Stevens.

Everyone in the team lived in Shakespeare Street. It was called Even Stevens because all the players lived in houses or flats with even numbers. They played their matches on the Astroturf behind the Mammoth Hypermarket.

From *Even Stevens F.C.* by Michael Rosen

Reading

1. Choose one of the settings. What do you think might happen in the story? Make some notes.

2. What other settings might there be in the story? Make notes.

Writing

1. Write your own short description of the school playground.

PCM 4

2. Read it to your partner. Compare your descriptions.

3. Discuss what might happen next in your story. Write a sentence which will make your partner want to read on.

Extended Writing

Plan and write the rest of your story. Include a good description of the setting.

Don't forget!

SETTINGS:

- vivid details
- descriptive words and phrases
- synonyms
- make it real

REPORT

Cat Speak

A cat tells you how he feels by miaowing and purring, and by the way he moves his body. Here are some clues to what he might be saying to you.

1 *Hi there!*

To say hello, your cat miaows loudly and rubs his fur against you.

present tense

sub-heading

3 *Purrfectly happy!*

2 Most cats really enjoy a tickle behind their ears.

He might also lick your skin and push his claws into you.

4 Cats rub against you to leave their smell on you.

A happy cat purrs loudly and stretches out somewhere warm and comfortable with his eyes half-closed.

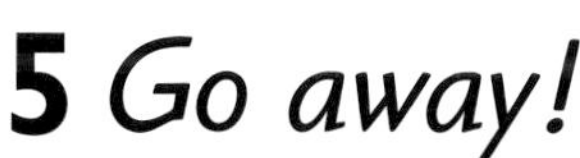

5 *Go away!*

Cats want to keep other cats off their territory. To scare them away, a cat puffs up his body and makes himself look bigger. If he's very angry he hisses and spits.

So you see, although your cat can't speak, he can tell you lots of things. ← summary

Reading

1. Answer the questions on **sheet 5**. Use the **Cat Speak** report to help you.
2. What do you think the cat is saying in box 2? Think of a sub-heading.

Writing

Work with a partner.

1. Plan a short report using headings and sub-headings. Look for more information from books if you need to.
2. Draft a short introduction.
3. Write a few sentences about each sub-heading.

PCM 7

Extended Writing

1. Finish drafting your report together. Write a short summary at the end.
2. Read your draft report to another pair.
3. Check clarity and spelling and revise it.

- present tense
- introduction
- headings and sub-headings
- summary at the end

4

DIALOGUE

Harry's Party

Chris Powling

When Sareeka's invitation arrived, I knew at once who I wanted to be.

'Robocop?' said Mum. 'Why do you want to go as Robocop?'

'He's half-cop, half-robot, Mum. In a film I saw advertised on TV, he goes round zapping everybody really hard!'

punctuation

Reading

1. Think about Harry's mum giving Harry the costume. What does she say? What does Harry say? Write two speech bubbles.
2. Write the speech as punctuated dialogue using speech marks.
3. Write some more lines of dialogue between Harry and his mum.

Writing

Look at the dialogue between Harry and his dad on **sheet 9**.

Write it out without speech bubbles or pictures.

Make it clear who is speaking.

She did, too.

Extended Writing

What happens when Harry meets his baby sister?

Write some dialogue between Harry and his parents.

DIALOGUE:

- "speech marks"
- no speech marks in bubbles
- capital letters at the beginning
- punctuation after speech
- new line for new speaker

5

PLAYSCRIPT

Ace Dragon Ltd

A play adapted from the story by Russell Hoban

Scene 1

John is walking down a street when he hears something go KLONK. He looks down and sees a round iron cover, with ***Ace Dragon Ltd*** *written on it. He stamps on it and hears a voice from underground.*

Ace: Who is it?
John: John.
Ace: (*Grumpily*) What do you want?
John: I want to know what Ltd means.
Ace: It means limited.
John: What does limited mean?
Ace: It means I can't do everything. I can only do some things.
John: What can you do?
Ace: I can make fire come out of my nose and mouth. I can fly. I can spin gold into straw if you have any gold.
John: I don't have any gold.
Ace: Do you need any straw?
John: No!
Ace: Then it doesn't matter. Do you want to go flying with me?
John: (*Excitedly*) Yes I do.
Ace: Then you have to come down and fight me. If you win, I'll take you flying.

(John pulls the iron cover but it doesn't move)

John: I can't lift this iron cover. It's too heavy. Can you lift it?
Ace: Take the Underground to Dragonham East. I'll meet you there.

Ace Dragon Ltd *from the story by Russell Hoban*

John said, 'I didn't know you ran out of petrol.'
Ace said, 'That's how I make my fire and that's what makes me go.'
John said, 'Can't we glide back down to earth?'
Ace said, 'No we can't. If I stop flapping my wings we'll crash.'
5 John said, 'Look! Can you get as far as that little golden moon?'
Ace said, 'I'll try.'

They landed on the moon just as Ace ran out of petrol.

John said, 'We could jump back down to earth if we had something soft to land on.'
Ace said, 'Yes, but we don't.'
10 John said, 'This is a golden moon,' and he sliced off some gold with his sword.
John said to Ace, 'If you can spin some gold into straw, you can make something soft for us to land on.'

Ace spun the gold into straw, then John sliced off more gold and Ace spun more straw. Ace and John made a great bundle of straw. Then they held on to the bundle
15 and they jumped.

Reading

1. Work in pairs. Decide who will read the parts of John and Ace Dragon.
2. Think about how you will read the lines. Mark the playscript on **sheet 11**.
3. Read the scene through together. What actions will you make? Make notes on the sheet.

Writing

1. Write the rest of the story (lines 8–15) as a playscript. Use **sheet 13**.
2. What happens next? Write some more lines of dialogue for John and Ace.

Extended Writing

Plan another adventure for John and the Dragon. Make it into a short play.

REPORT

People and Places

My Favourite Person

present tense

My grandad is a small fat man. He is very kind and jolly.

On Saturday morning he listens to the radio and sings with me.

My grandad loves walking, and he takes me walking in the woods. He tells me all about the trees and flowers in the wood. My grandad likes reading and listens to me read. But there is one thing. He is a terrible snorer!!!! The bed shakes and the windows clatter, when my grandad snores.

Grandad is a funny man. He tells lots of jokes and makes people laugh.

Neil, age 8

My Favourite Place

introduction

Flamborough is on the East coast near Bridlington. It has a lovely lighthouse and is my favourite place. I like to go there with my family.

group facts

There's lots to do at Flamborough. The best things are looking for crabs in rock pools and exploring the caves. One cave is as big as a cathedral. Another cave is a smugglers cave. A fisherman told me that a long time ago smugglers hid inside it.

Sometimes people get stuck in the caves and on the cliffs and helicopters come and rescue them. It's exciting, but not for those people.

A lot of birds, like puffins and seagulls, nest in the rocks outside the caves. They make a lot of noise in the day and in the early morning.

Karen, age 9

Reading

1 Look again at Neil's report. What do you know about Neil's grandad? Pick out the key words. Write them on the word web on **sheet 14**.

2 Make notes about Flamborough on **sheet 15**.

Writing

1 Carry on writing the report. Use the notes from shared writing to help you.

2 Write your own introduction, or add the one from shared writing.

Extended Writing

Finish your report. Read it aloud to someone else.

Which part do they like best? What could be improved? Make any changes.

- introduction
- present tense
- group similar facts together

7

SHAPE POEMS

Rhythm Machine

Soft and humming

and

strumming

Listen to that **NEAT** refrain!

Add a

Stanley Cook

Stanley Cook

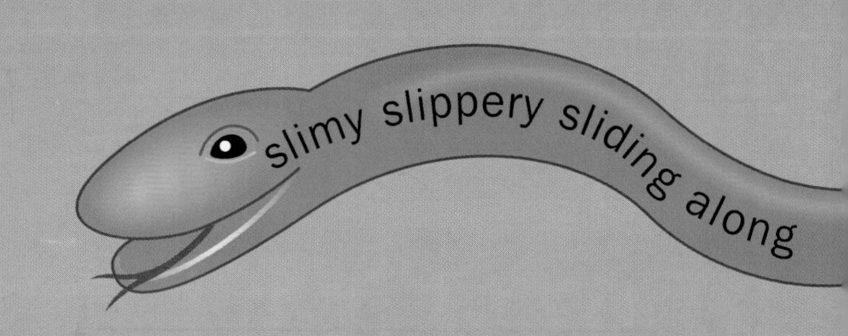

And a

kit

Why not change the B E A T again?

UP THE VOLUME

Eardrum priser,

POP GROUP
syntheSIZER!

Trevor Harvey

the ground in and out of the grass...

Reading

1. Work with a partner. Which is your favourite word shape poem? Talk about why you like it best. Make notes.
2. Make up word shapes for ball, banana and flower.

Writing

PCM 18

1. Brainstorm some words for your own calligram poem.
2. Work on each word to make it look like what it means.

- Use shape, size and colour.

Extended Writing

Use your best ideas to make a calligram poem. Make a final copy for a class collection

Frogs and Toads

Spot the difference!

	FROG	TOAD
Skin	smooth, yellowish brown, moist	dry, rough, bumpy, greyish brown
Head	narrow, pointed near mouth	short and broad flat
Eyes	see all way round	see all way round
Tongue	long, very sticky tip	long, very sticky tip
Body	slim middle bit	fat middle
Legs	long at back, strong	shorter, fat, strong
Movement	hops, jumps, leaps	crawls, walks

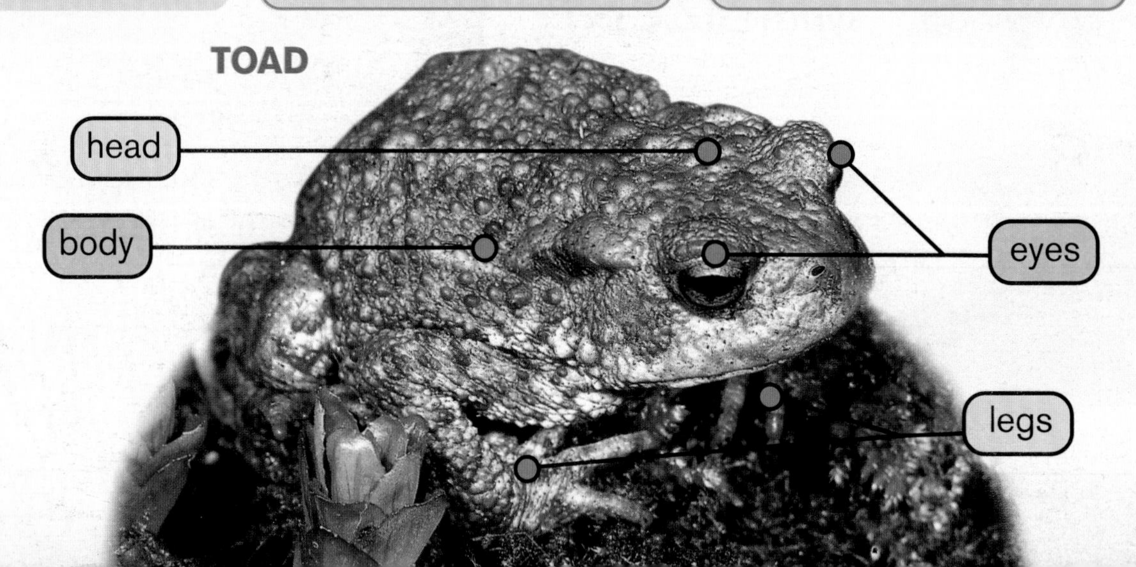

The Toad Fact Tree

What they look like
dry Skin rough bumpy
Short body grey-brown
flat head
Short Sturdy back legs
tongue joined to front
of mouth - Sticky
no teeth

Food
Spiders bugs
insects

Movement
crawl walk
Short hops

Life Cycle
eggs - long Strings
covered in jelly
Laid in Water
change into
tadpoles
- toads

Where they live
Land - gardens fields
mainly woods
ponds to lay eggs

Reading

1. Look at the information about frogs. Make a labelled picture of a frog. Use **sheet 19**.

2. Fill in the Fact Web about toads on **sheet 20**. Then finish writing the short report about toads.

Writing

1. Brainstorm information about the second subject.
2. Write key facts on the chart on **sheet 21**.
3. Add the key facts about the first subject from shared writing.
4. Discuss ways of presenting your information.

Extended Writing

1. Decide on the best way to present your information.
2. Make an information sheet about your topic.
3. Try to include labelled pictures on your final copy.

INFORMATION:

- key facts
- headings
- pictures or diagrams
- think about the layout

REPEATING PHRASES

Like and Hate

Tomato 1

Here's me
and my mum's just given me
a tomato.
And if there's one thing
I can't stand
it's tomatoes.
You know that fleshy bit
the way it sticks to your teeth
and you know all those slimy little seeds,
the way they slide around your mouth
ooh
I can't stand it.

Anyway,
my mum says,
Eat it.
And I say,
Don't want to.
She says,
Eat it.
And I say,
I hate tomatoes, all slimy …

Michael Rosen

Tomato 2: or how I've learnt to love tomatoes

When I get in
if there's one thing I love
it's a fat red tomato.
I love the feel of my tongue and lips
on the tight skin.
Then I make my teeth
cut into the flesh
so the juice jumps into my mouth
the coolness
and
the wetness.
So now I get some salt
and put a few grains on the flesh
so with my next bite
a tasty feel starts under my tongue …

Michael Rosen

Battle Lines

What I hate about spiders
Is their great big black hairy legs.

What I like about spiders
Is the way they spin such beautiful silky webs.

What I hate about spiders
Is the way they hide in corners
And creep up on you
When you least expect it.

What I like about spiders
Is the way they make some people scream
When you put them down their backs.

What I hate about spiders
Is when you're in the bath
And turn on the tap –
They come tumbling out on top of you.

What I like about spiders
Is the way they never give up.
They keep coming up the plughole.
Even when you've washed them down.

Sandy Brownjohn

Reading

Work with a partner.

1. Choose your favourite poem. Practise reading it aloud. Make it sound like someone talking.

2. How many verbs can you think of to describe eating? Use a thesaurus to help you.

chew
guzzle

Writing

Write your own 'Hate/Like' poem.
Use **sheet 22**.
Use a thesaurus to help you find the best words.

Extended Writing

1. Finish writing your poem.
   Swap it with a partner.
   Are the feelings really strong?

2. Revise the poem and write out a final version for a class display.

- like and hate pattern
- powerful verbs
- descriptive adjectives
- always try to find the right word

STORY OPENINGS AND ENDINGS

Once Upon a Time ... the End

Opening 1

Josie could do many tricks. She could balance a pencil on the end of her finger. She could pick her nose without anyone seeing. She could tickle the cat until it said Stop it! But her best trick happened at 10.30 one Friday morning. It was a trick that changed her life.

It happened in the school playground when Billy Brand got his head stuck in the school railings.

Opening 2

"I'm going to make something special for your mother," my father said.

My mother was out shopping. My father was in the kitchen looking at the pots and pans and the jars of this and that.

"What are you going to make?" I said.

"A pudding," he said.

My father is a big man with wild black hair. When he laughs, the sun laughs in the window-panes. When he thinks, you can almost see his thoughts sitting on the tables and chairs. When he is angry, me and my little brother Huey shiver to the bottom of our shoes.

dialogue

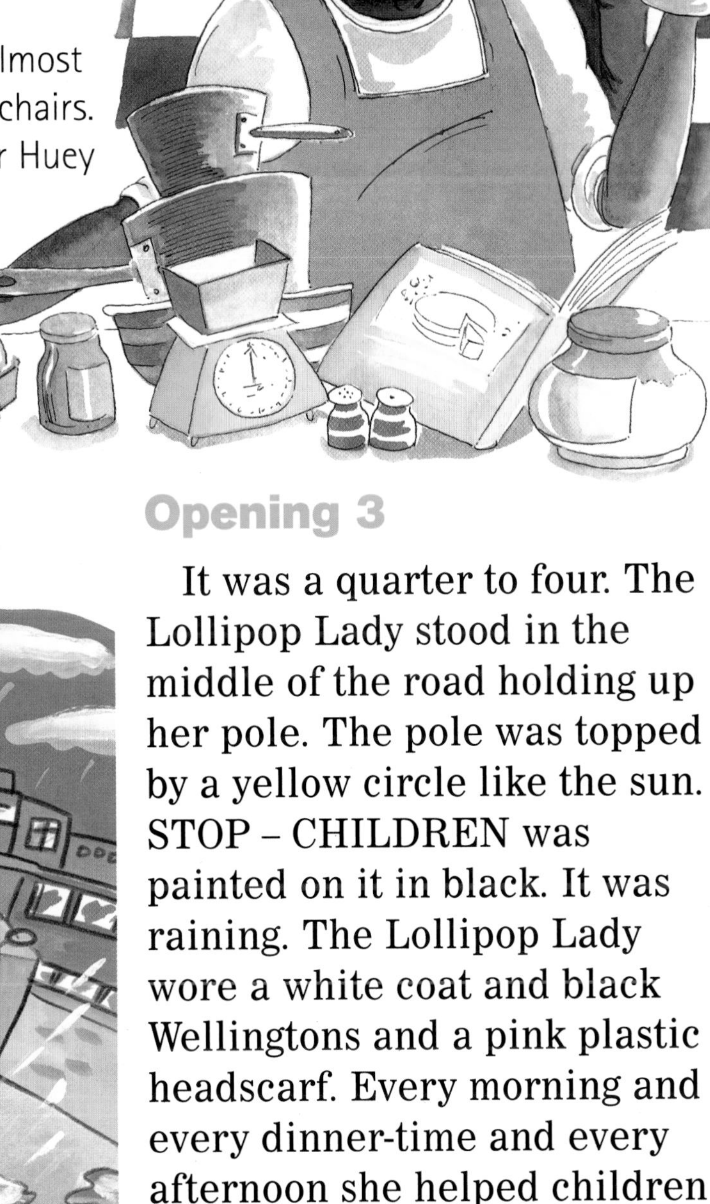

Opening 3

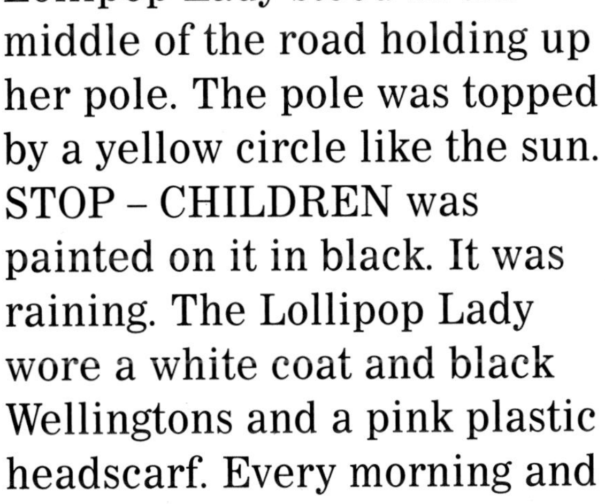

It was a quarter to four. The Lollipop Lady stood in the middle of the road holding up her pole. The pole was topped by a yellow circle like the sun. STOP – CHILDREN was painted on it in black. It was raining. The Lollipop Lady wore a white coat and black Wellingtons and a pink plastic headscarf. Every morning and every dinner-time and every afternoon she helped children to cross the road outside Rylands Primary School.

Reading

Work with a partner.

1. Read the story endings on **sheet 23**. Match them to the right opening.

2. What do you think happened in between? Make notes for one story.

Writing

1. Write your own story opening. Use one of the models to help you.
2. Quickly plot the story. What will happen? How will it end?
3. Write a good ending.

PCM 25

Extended Writing

Write some more story openings and endings. You can base them on the other stories here.

STORY PLANNING

Who? What? Where?

By Jason

Story board

Important words needed

Spaceship
Alien
Landed
moon
men
about
Started crying

By Vicky

Reading

With a partner, look at the two plans.

1. What does each plan tell you? Fill in the chart on **sheet 26**.

2. What is good about the plans? What could be better? Make notes about each one.

Writing

Plan your own story. Use **sheet 28** to help you. You can make notes or drawings.

Extended Writing

Use one of the other planning methods to plan a different story.
Which way works best?

- main characters
- setting
- events
- beginning, middle and end

12

CHARACTER

A Poor Widow's Son

Once upon a time there was a king who had a daughter. She was as beautiful as a sunny day. Her mother the queen had died when she was a baby. Her stepmother, the new queen, was jealous of her because she was more beautiful than her own daughter.

typical adjectives

Long ago there was a handsome prince who went out into the world to seek his fortune. After he had travelled for many days he came one night to a giant's castle. He knocked on the door to ask for work, and the giant took him in. "I am an easy master if you do as you're told, but if you disobey me, I will kill you," said the giant.

Once there was a poor widow's son, who wanted to marry the king's daughter. He set off cheerfully towards the palace, but on the way he met a tall stranger dressed in red, with feet like a goat's. "Can I help you?" smiled the stranger.

Reading

Work with a partner.

1. Think of some adjectives for each of the characters on **sheet 29**.
2. Write them down on the character web.
3. Choose another character from a story. Make a new character web for him or her.

Writing

Work on your own.

1. Make a 'Wanted' poster for a baddy. Use **sheet 31**.
2. Make a 'Missing' poster for a goody. Use **sheet 32**.
3. Show your poster to your partner. How could you make it better?

Extended Writing

Make a finished copy of your poster for a Goodies and Baddies Gallery.

NOTE MAKING

Memo to me

snail small
tentics stretch
eyes glow
moves slowly through
grass
careful
big blackbird in the air
coming to eat you

The Snail

The snail, the snail
How small he is with
Tenticles that stretch and
Eyes that glow
Shivering like snow.

Slowly it moves through the grass,
Careful, careful ...
Who goes there?
It's me noiseless snail.
"I'm a big blackbird," said
He in the air.
"Coming to eat you
Beware, beware."

by Justin, age 8

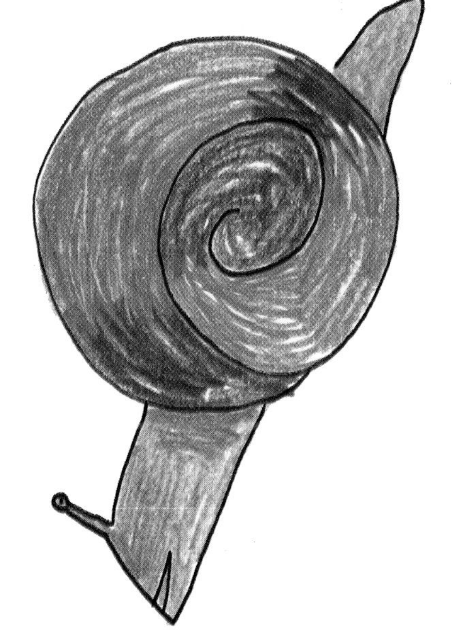

Reading

Work with a partner. Use **sheet 33**.

1. Read what a pupil said about his friend.
2. Underline the key words.
3. Cross out words which aren't important.

Writing

Work with a partner. Use **sheet 34** if it's helpful.

1. Tell your partner about yourself – your family, your interests, what you like and what you don't like. Your partner makes notes.
2. When your teacher tells you to stop, swap.

Extended Writing

Use your notes to write character descriptions of each other.
Make them into a class book called 'Read All About Us'.

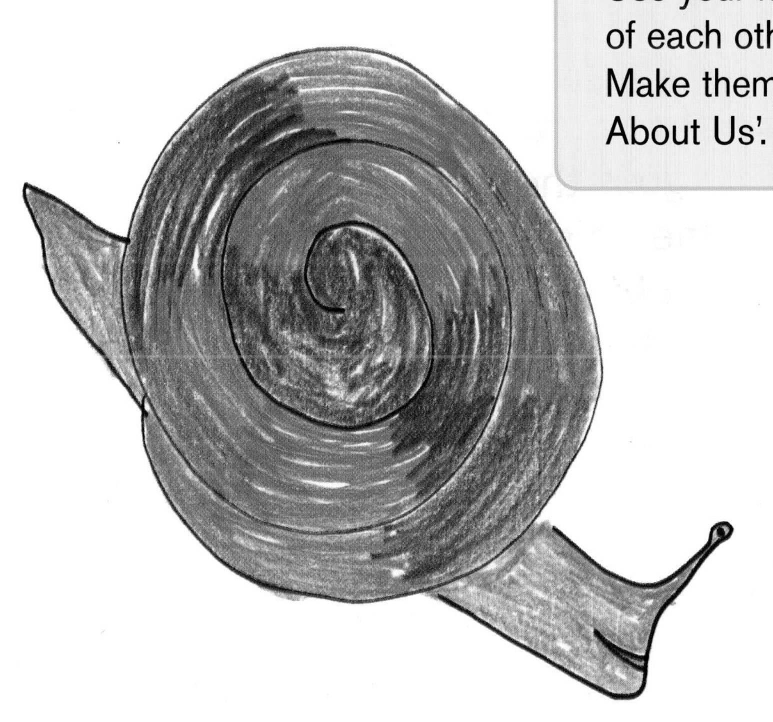

Don't forget!

NOTES:

- key words and phrases
- key facts
- don't have to be sentences

14

STORY MAPS

Jack's Journey

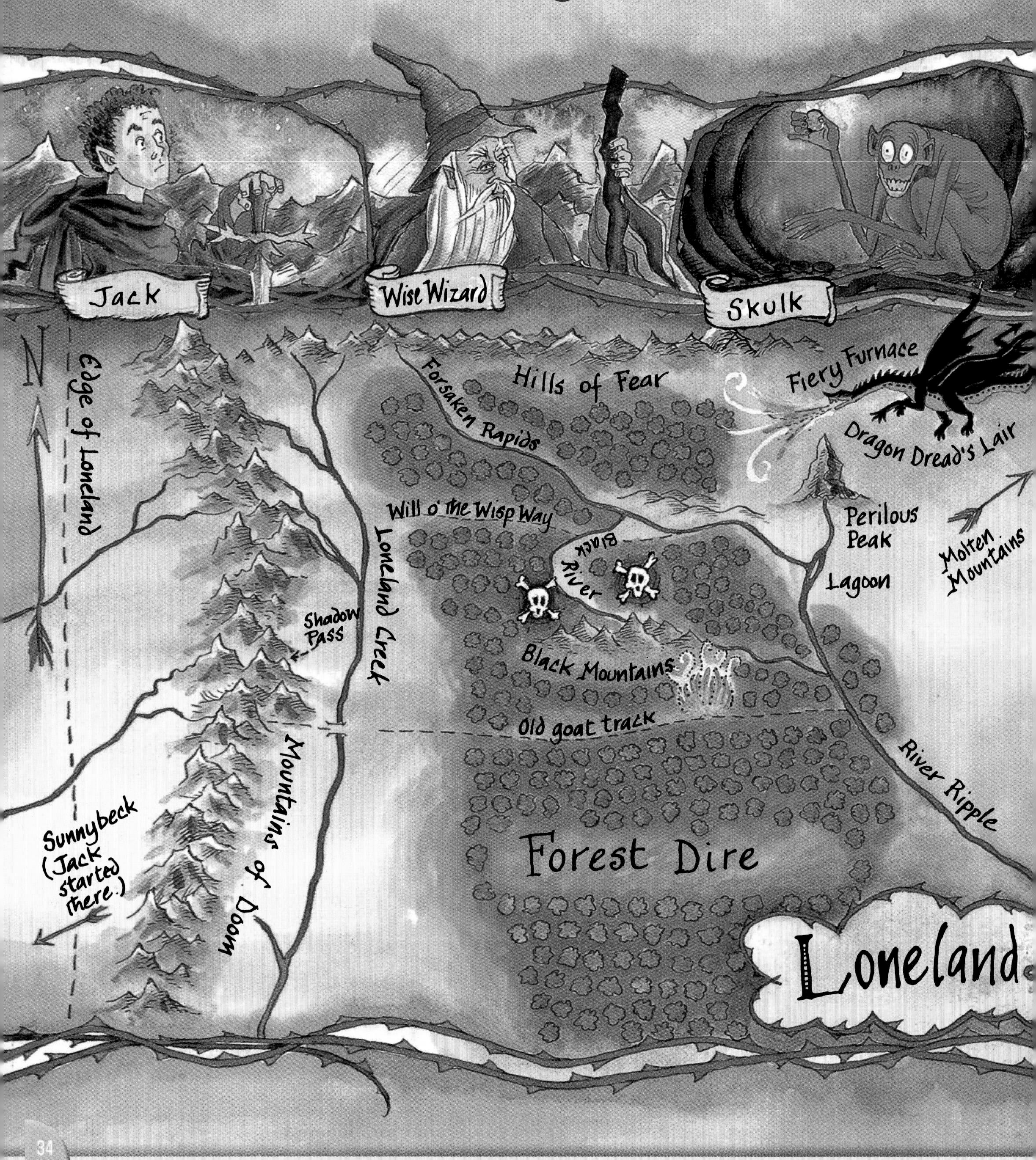

Jack's Journey

Story outline

Jack is a poor but brave boy who goes to look for treasure. The terrible Dragon Dread guards the treasure. The Wise Wizard goes with Jack. They climb the Mountains of Doom. They meet:

- evil trolls
- will o' the wisps

and face the Forsaken Rapids.

Jack finds a copper coin which gives him secret powers.

Later on Jack:

- meets the nasty Skulk
- crosses the Black River
- climbs Perilous Peak to escape his enemies.

He fights Dragon Dread with the help of his magic powers and the Wise Wizard.

Jack wins!

Reading

Work with a partner.

1. Read the story outline of ***Jack's Journey*** together.
2. Look at the map. Work out which way Jack might have gone. Using **sheet 35** plan his route from Sunnybeck to Dragon Dread's Lair.
3. Where might some of the adventures have happened? Label them on the map.

Writing

Work with a partner.

1. Choose a story about a journey.
2. What are the main events? Where do they happen?
3. Draw a rough map. Label it with an arrow to each place.
4. You could invent places where other adventures happen. Label them on the map.

Extended Writing

Practise telling your story to a partner, using the map to help you. Talk about how you could improve the map. Make a final copy.

15 RULES

Hamsters must not ...

Hamsters must not

- chew the bars on the cage
- chew electric wires
- dig up the carpet
- eat fingers
- poo on the carpet
- leave food on the carpet

Ellen age 7

Hamsters must

- learn how to keep the cage clean
- learn how to get up in the daytime

verbs at the beginning

ANIMAL SAFARI

A game for two, three or four people

2nd person

YOU WILL NEED

- Dice
- A different coloured counter for each player

RULES

1. Each player throws the dice. The highest score goes first.
2. Throw the dice.
3. Move that number of squares from the start.
4. If you land on 'Danger' you miss a turn.
5. If you land on any instructions, DO WHAT THEY SAY!!
6. The person who gets to the Safari Lodge first is the winner.

MIND HOW YOU YO!

1 Always yo away from other people.
2 Keep your yo-yo away from your face and eyes.
3 Never look down on the yo-yo.
4 Never throw a spin at other people.
5 Make sure your string is in good condition.
6 Never use a damaged yo-yo.
7 Never use yo-yos in classrooms or corridors.

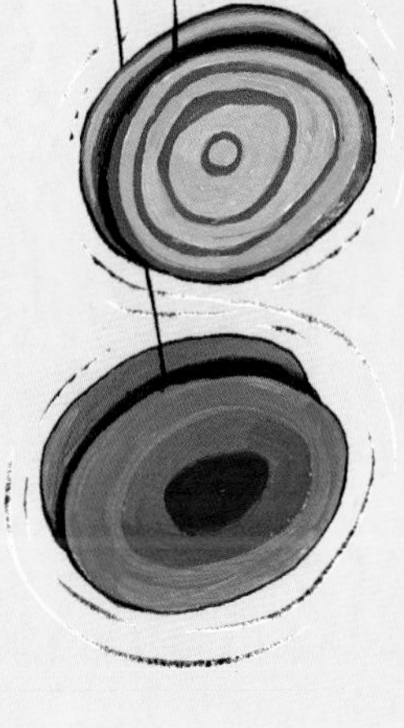

Yo safely – and have fun!

numbered points

Reading

Look at the notes again.

1 Answer questions 1–3 on **sheet 36**.

2 Complete all the activities on **sheet 36**.

- verbs at the beginning
- 2nd person
- clear and simple
- bullet points or numbers

Writing

Look at the playground scene on **sheet 37**.

1 Draft some more rules for people at the playground.

2 Read them aloud to a partner. Are they clear? Make any changes.

3 How will you set out your rules? Write them out neatly.

Extended Writing

Finish writing your rules. Illustrate them. Show what **could** happen if they are not followed.

TRADITIONAL TALE/PARABLE

Too Much Searching

A MAN WENT IN TO THE BUSH TO CUT WOOD. As he passed along the way he looked at one tree and then another, but he did not see the one he wanted to cut. In time he came to a high rocky place, and up above he saw a good tree growing. So he climbed the hill and started to cut. But there was a rock lying where he wanted to stand. He rolled the rock away and cut the tree.

The rock that he had moved rolled downward. It bounded into a clump of bushes where a small antelope was resting. The frightened antelope

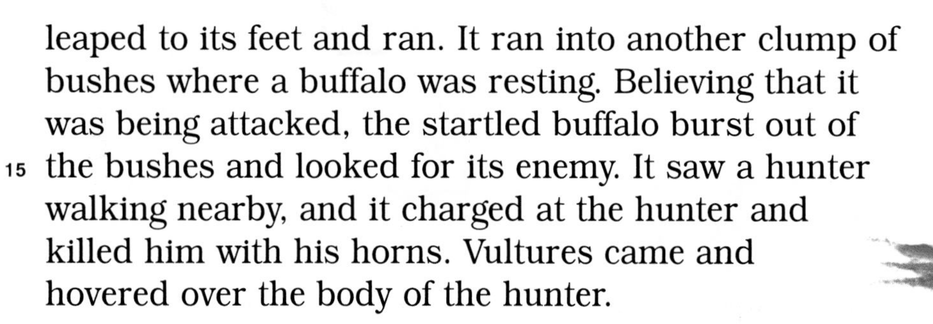

leaped to its feet and ran. It ran into another clump of bushes where a buffalo was resting. Believing that it was being attacked, the startled buffalo burst out of the bushes and looked for its enemy. It saw a hunter walking nearby, and it charged at the hunter and killed him with his horns. Vultures came and hovered over the body of the hunter.

In the village, people saw the hovering vultures, and they went out to see what was there. They found the body of the hunter. They asked one another: "What caused this man to die?" They saw the hoofprints of the buffalo and asked: "What caused the buffalo to come and kill this person?" They followed the hoofprints of the buffalo and came to the clump of bushes where it had been resting.

There they discovered the hoofprints of the small antelope. They said: "Ah! The buffalo was surprised by the coming of the antelope. But what caused the antelope to enter where the buffalo was lying?" They followed the prints of the antelope to the first clump of bushes, saying, "Yes, here the antelope came out. But what caused him to do so?" They found the rock there, and saw the marks it had made rolling down from the high place. They said: "It is clear. A rock disturbed it. But what caused the rock to enter here where the antelope was resting?"

They followed the trail of the rock and came to where the tree had been cut. They said: "Why, a man cut a tree here, and he moved the rock to do his work."

They went home. They discussed everything. They said: "When the sun rose, everything was peaceful. The land was quiet. The man went to cut wood. He passed many trees that would have been suitable. But he went to a different place and found a tree there. The trees he passed, he could have had any of them. Everything would have remained peaceful. But he went to a high place. He moved the rock. He disturbed things that were lying quietly. As a result, one thing happened, then another, and the hunter died."

So the people made a proverb

"Too much searching disturbs things that are lying still."

lesson at end

Reading

Work with a partner.

1. Tell the story to each other. Make sure you get each bit in the right order.
2. Fill in the story chain on **sheet 38**.

Writing

Work with a partner. Plan your own parable.

1. Make notes about the **setting**, **characters** and **main events**.
2. Start to fill in the story chain plan on **sheet 40**.
3. Write the lesson at the end of the story.

Extended Writing

Write the first draft of your parable. Follow your story chain plan. Revise your work, looking out for the spelling of plurals.

Don't forget!

- small events lead to bigger events
- final disaster
- unravel the story
- lesson at the end

17

SEQUEL

Mighty Mountain

typical opening

MANY YEARS AGO in a small village in Japan, a huge baby was born. He was so big that everyone called him Baby Mountain.

By the time he was twelve, he was the biggest, strongest boy in the school and the wrestling champion of the whole village. The people of the village called him Mighty Mountain.

One warm autumn day, Mighty Mountain decided he would go to the city and become a famous wrestler.

It was a long walk to the city and Mighty Mountain strode along. Then he noticed a girl filling her bucket with water. She was very pretty, with pink cheeks, shining black hair and sparkling eyes.

Mighty Mountain thought it would be fun to make her spill the water. He crept up behind the girl and poked a giant finger in her side. The girl squeaked and giggled, but she didn't spill the water. Then, she trapped his massive hand under her arm.

Mighty Mountain tried to pull his hand away, but it wouldn't budge.

'Let me go,' he laughed. 'You're very strong for a girl, but I don't want to hurt you.'

But the harder he pulled, the tighter the girl's grip seemed to get. She began to walk on, dragging the wrestler behind her.

'Please let me go,' he begged. 'I'm Mighty Mountain, and I'm on my way to the city to become a famous wrestler.'

'Oh, you must come and meet Grandma, then. You seem tired. She can help you.'

'I don't need help from you,' roared Mighty Mountain, but he was feeling tired. If he refused to go with the girl, she might easily break his arm. He nodded and the girl let him go.

They came at last to a small thatched hut high up in the mountains. Round the corner of the hut came the girl's mother carrying a cow on 35 her shoulders.

'Who is this nice young man, Kuniko?'

Kuniko told her.

'Mm,' said Mother, 'he looks delicate. He needs some proper food.'

40 Then Kuniko called Grandma.

A tiny, wrinkled, toothless old lady shuffled out, leaning heavily on a stick. She stumbled over the roots of the great oak tree in the yard.

'Ow ... ow ... ow ...' she muttered. 'That's 45 the third time this week I've bumped into that silly old tree.'

She put her thin arms round the trunk and pulled it straight out of the ground.

'Throw it away, dear,' she said to her 50 daughter.

Kuniko's mother threw the tree. It flew through the air like a rocket, getting smaller and smaller until it landed on a far mountainside.

Mighty Mountain could stand no more. With 55 a terrific thump, he crumpled to the ground.

Mighty Mountain had fainted.

opposites

Retold by Irene Hedlund

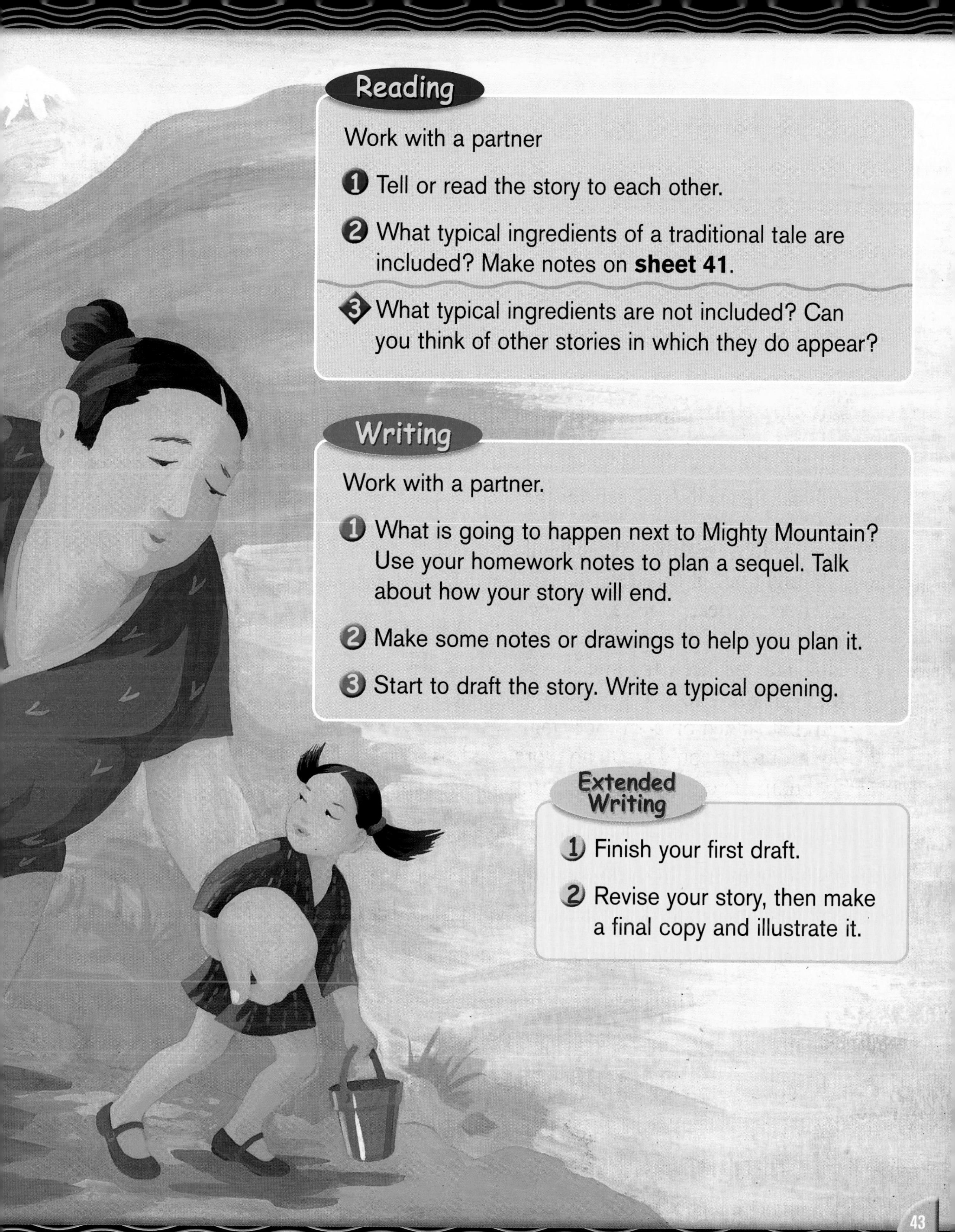

Reading

Work with a partner

1. Tell or read the story to each other.
2. What typical ingredients of a traditional tale are included? Make notes on **sheet 41**.
3. What typical ingredients are not included? Can you think of other stories in which they do appear?

Writing

Work with a partner.

1. What is going to happen next to Mighty Mountain? Use your homework notes to plan a sequel. Talk about how your story will end.
2. Make some notes or drawings to help you plan it.
3. Start to draft the story. Write a typical opening.

Extended Writing

1. Finish your first draft.
2. Revise your story, then make a final copy and illustrate it.

INSTRUCTIONS

How to ...

Recycled paper

YOU WILL NEED

- *Old paper*
- *Bucket*
- *Water*
- *Paper towel*
- *Newspaper*
- *Plastic lid (such as an ice-cream tub)*
- *Pair of tights*

Stage 1

- Rip the paper into small pieces.
- Put the paper in a bucket with water.
- Stir the small pieces up in the bucket.
- Squash it with your hands.
- Leave for a week.

Stage 2

- Make holes in a plastic lid to make a sieve.
- Stretch a pair of tights over the sieve.
- Pour the contents of the bucket through the sieve.
- Leave for about a minute.

Peanut butter cookies

YOU WILL NEED

- 75g butter
- 50g peanut butter
- 100g caster sugar
- 100g soft brown sugar
- 1 egg
- 150g flour
- 1/4 of a level teaspoon of salt

1. Switch on the oven and heat to 190°C/ gas mark 5.
2. Mix the butter, peanut butter, sugar and egg together in a bowl.
3. Add the flour and salt, and mix to a fine dough.

4. Make the dough into 36 balls.
5. Place the dough balls onto a baking tray.
6. Flatten them with a fork, making a criss-cross pattern.

Stage 3

- Get the paper towel and newspaper.
- Flip the mixture on to the paper towel and newspaper.
- Press the paper towel on the mixture.
- Wait for your recycled paper to dry.

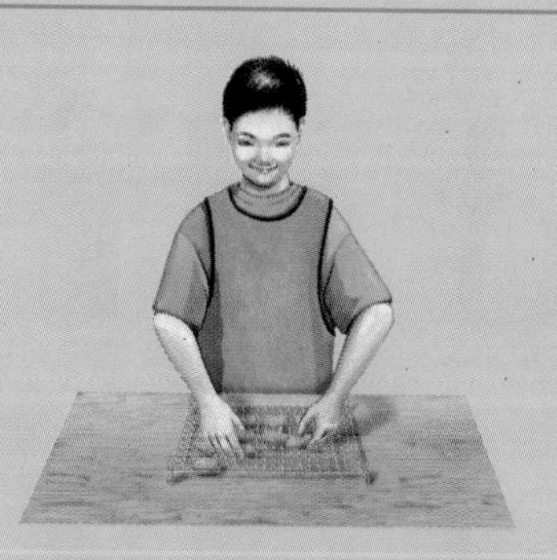

7 Bake in the oven for 10–12 minutes, until golden brown.

8 Cool on trays and store in an airtight container.

Reading

Look at the instructions with a partner. Answer the questions on **sheet 42**.

Writing

1. Draft a set of instructions for a class book called *How to Survive on Earth: A Guide for Aliens.*
2. Add diagrams or pictures to make your instructions clear.

PCM 44

- purpose and reader
- clear instructions
- numbered steps
- verbs at the beginning
- diagrams or pictures

Extended Writing

1. Finish writing your set of instructions.
2. Swap with a partner, and read aloud each other's work. Are the steps in the right order?
3. Make a final copy for the class book.

Getting to the Point

Daisy
Kate S rang 11am.
BBQ her house
1pm tomorrow.
If can go
ring 8865432
after 4.
Dad

C
Sandwich in fridge
gone shopping
back 6'ish
Mum
X
P.S I fed pickles

Shark Spotted off Cornish Coast

Benjie – to do!
feed fish
take gerbil to Jake's
Pack bag
Kite
body board
flippers
Snorkel
Wet-suit
Post Gran's b/day card
Comics/books/pencils

Reading

Use **sheet 45**.

1. Write out Dad's message to Daisy in full sentences.
2. What is the purpose of each message? Underline the best word.
3. What is the headline about? Write one or two sentences about it.

Writing

1. Read the text from shared writing. Underline the key points and make notes.
2. Read another non-fiction text. Underline the key points and make notes.

This is a great story Han Su!
Exciting ending!
But – no speech marks.

Extended Writing

1. Finish making notes on each section of the report.
2. Talk through each section with a partner. Then write out the main ideas of the passage, in your own words.

20

TRADITIONAL POEM

The Hairy Toe

Once there was a woman who went out to pick beans,
and she found a Hairy Toe.
She took the Hairy Toe home with her,
and that night, when she went to bed,
the wind began to moan and groan.
Away off in the distance
she seemed to hear a voice crying.
'Where's my Hair-r-ry To-o-oe?
Who's got my Hair-r-ry To-o-oe?'

The woman scrooched down,
way down under the covers,
and about that time
the wind appeared to hit the house,

smoosh,

and the old house creaked and cracked
like something was trying to get in.
The voice had come nearer,
almost at the door now,
and it said,
'Where's my Hair-r-ry To-o-oe?
Who's got my Hair-r-ry To-o-oe?'

The woman scrooched further down
under the covers
and pulled them tight around her head.

The wind growled around the house
like some big animal
and r-r-um-umbled
over the chimney.
All at once she heard the door cr-r-a-ack
and Something slipped in
and began to creep over the floor.

The floor went
cre-e-eak, cre-e-eak
at every step that thing took towards her bed.
The woman could almost feel
it bending over her bed.
There in an awful voice it said:
'Where's my Hair-r-ry To-o-oe?
Who's got my Hair-r-ry To-o-oe?
You've got it!'

Reading

Work with your group.

1. Decide who will read which bits of the poem.
2. How will you read it? Loudly? Softly? Slowly? Think about how it will sound.
3. Practise reading the poem aloud. Add some sound effects. Make it sound scary!

Writing

Work with a partner.

1. What happens next? Write some extra lines for the poem.
2. Try reading the lines aloud as you write. What sounds could you add?

PCM 48

Extended Writing

1. Finish writing your extra lines. Write out a final version of the whole poem.
2. Illustrate the poem for a class display.

Don't forget!

- soft and loud voices
- powerful verbs
- sound effects
- make it scary

21

SUMMARY

Sea World

If you looked down at the Earth from Space, you would see that most of our planet is covered by water. Nearly three quarters of the Earth is covered in water. This huge amount of water is separated by land into five areas. These are called oceans.

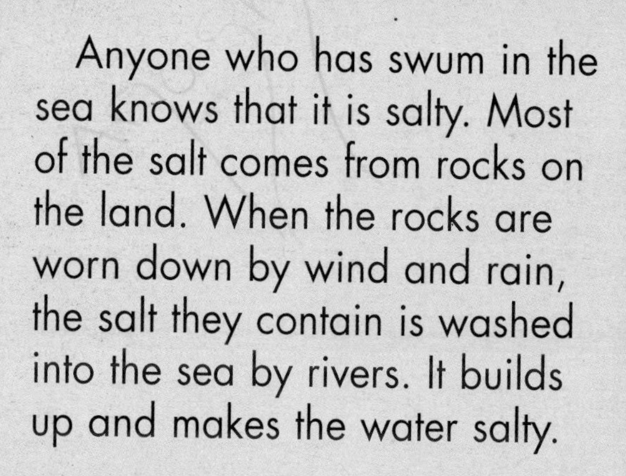

Anyone who has swum in the sea knows that it is salty. Most of the salt comes from rocks on the land. When the rocks are worn down by wind and rain, the salt they contain is washed into the sea by rivers. It builds up and makes the water salty.

The sea is never still. Waves and tides keep the water moving. Most waves are made by the wind. The stronger the wind, the bigger the waves. Twice a day, the time comes in and goes out. At high tide, the water moves further onto the land and at low tide it moves away from the land.

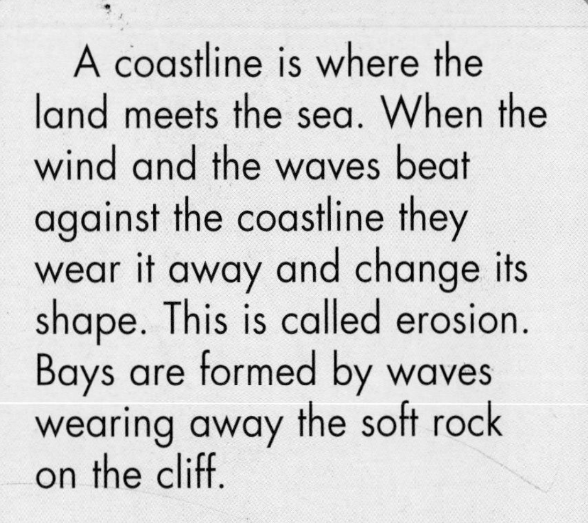

A coastline is where the land meets the sea. When the wind and the waves beat against the coastline they wear it away and change its shape. This is called erosion. Bays are formed by waves wearing away the soft rock on the cliff.

Strong waves cause big rocks to fall away from the land into the sea. They knock against each other and break up into smaller rocks. Eventually, tiny bits of broken up rock and shell turn into grains of sand.

All the animals in the sea need food. Many of the smaller creatures eat sea plants, and bigger animals hunt and eat the smaller sea creatures. They are then eaten by even larger animals. To stay alive in the sea, animals must find food and hide and protect themselves in different ways.

Reading

1. Read paragraph 4. What are the key words? Jot them down.
2. Talk about the main point of the paragraph. Use one sentence to say what it is about.
3. Do the same for paragraph 5.

4. Do the same for paragraph 6.

Writing

1. Read paragraph 2 of **Creatures of the Deep** on **sheet 50**. Underline the main points.
2. Write a sentence or two saying what it is about.

3. Do the same for paragraph 3.

Extended Writing

1. Read **Sea World** through again.
2. Write a summary of it, using no more than 50 words.

Don't forget!

- Pick out the key words.
- Think about what the paragraph is about.
- Summarise it in one or two sentences.

22

RECOUNT

The Market Street Mystery

3 Market Way
Platts Hill
Sussex PO32 4RF

Mrs Bates
Headteacher
Market Street School

3 March 2000

Dear Mrs Bates,

It is now two months since the school closed and our children are still going by bus to St James's Primary School. Many parents are very unhappy about this as it is affecting our children's education.

I am holding a meeting of concerned parents at my house this Thursday at 7pm. A member of the Council will be there and we will be asking her what they plan to do about it. We would like to invite you to attend.

Thank you for doing everything you can to help the children.

We hope to see you on Thursday.

Yours sincerely

Ruth Jones

Ruth Jones

Mystery Smell Closes School

By Gerald Williams

MARKET STREET SCHOOL was closed yesterday, after a teacher and two children became sick and dizzy, soon after entering the building. They all reported a strange metallic smell in their classroom.

The cause of the smell is not known, but experts say it seems to be coming from under the ground. They plan to drill a 30 metre deep hole to test old mine tunnels, under the school.

A parent said, "I'm not happy about the plans to 'bus' the children to a school three miles away. Something's got to be done – and soon."

Reading

1. Do the activities on **sheet 51**.
2. Who do you think will read each piece? Finish these sentences:

The newspaper report will be read by ....

The letter will be read by ....

Writing

Using the event from shared writing, either:

1. Plan and write a letter about the event. PCM 53

OR

2. Plan and write a newspaper report about the event. Include some speech. PCM 54

Extended Writing

1. Finish writing your letter or newspaper report.
2. Read it to your partner. Is it in the right style for the type of writing? Make any changes and check spelling and punctuation.

23

FIRST PERSON

DIARY OF A KILLER CAT

Anne Fine

MONDAY

OKAY, OKAY. So hang me. I killed the bird. For pity's sake, I'm a cat. It's practically my job to go creeping round the garden after sweet little eensy-weensy birdy-pies that can hardly fly from one hedge to another. So what am I supposed to do when one of the poor feathery little flutterballs just throws itself into my mouth? I mean, it practically landed on my paws. It could have hurt me.

Okay, okay. So I biffed it. Is that any reason for Ellie to cry in my fur so hard I almost drown, and squeeze me so hard I almost choke?

"Oh, Tuffy!" she says, all sniffles and red eyes and piles of wet tissues. "Oh, Tuffy. How could you do that?"

How could I do that? I'm a cat. How did I know there was going to be such a giant great fuss, with Ellie's mother rushing off to fetch sheets of old newspaper and Ellie's father filling a bucket with soapy water?

Okay, okay. So maybe I shouldn't have dragged it in and left it on the carpet. And maybe the stains won't come out, ever.

So hang me.

Reading

Work with a partner.

1. Read the **Diary of a Killer Cat** again.
2. Write a 3rd person account of what happened.

PCM 55

Writing

1. Read the story about Jake on **sheet 57**.
2. Write an entry for Jake's diary. Try to imagine how Jake feels. Make it chatty.

PCM 58

3. Start to write the next entry for Jake's diary. Write about his journey to the farm.

Don't forget!

1ST PERSON:

- I me my
- thoughts and feelings

Extended Writing

Carry on writing Jake's diary.
Invent some other adventures for him.

BOOK REVIEW

May We Recommend

Spider and Scorpion

I like this book because it tells you what spiders' insides look like and how they catch things and it shows all the different types of scorpions.

The pictures are very realistic. There are holes in the page and you can see the spiders' insides through the holes.

The best bit is how spiders catch things that are big like a tree frog. It was interesting about the relations of scorpions a long time ago. They were alive 500 million years ago.

I think scientists might like this book. My mum wouldn't like it but my Dad would. Other children would like this book if they weren't scared of spiders.

Tom

The Sheep Pig by Dick King-Smith

Babe isn't an ordinary pig. He wants to be a sheep pig. When he is put to the test he is a very special pig because he saves the sheep from being stolen.

Babe is a heart breaking story but it's funny too. It can really make you feel like you are there. I like Babe because he can talk and sing which makes me laugh. If you like animals you will love The Sheep Pig.

Narina

Reading

Work with a partner.

1. Read the reviews together. Fill in the chart on **sheet 59**.
2. Which review told you most about the book?

Writing

Work with a partner.

1. Write a book review of a story or a non-fiction book you have read.
2. Who would enjoy reading it? End your review with a recommendation.

Extended Writing

1. Revise and edit your review. Make a best copy for the library display.
2. Write a review of a different book.

Don't forget!

- title
- author/illustrator
- what it's about
- what you like or dislike
- who might enjoy it

LETTER

Dear Author

St Thomas More
RC PRIMARY SCHOOL

12.05.00

Dear Jamila Gavin,

I have read some of your books and I enjoyed them alot.

My favourite one of your books is 'I want to be an Angel' because it's got lots of stories in it about different children. We have read 'Grandpa Chatterji' in class and I loved it especially when he went to the fairground with Neetu and Sanja.

What was your childhood like in India? Did you like reading books when you were little? Where do you get ideas for your stories? Did you like England?

Yours sincerely

Francesca Turner

Francesca Turner

Throndale Road ▪ Belmont ▪ Durham ▪ DH1 2AQ

13 Mean Street
Blackdale
Devon

11th March 2000

Exotic Pets
Poppoff Place
Shinner HA5 2HR

Dear Sir or Madam

I am writing to ask you to send me your catalogue. I am hoping to buy a pet lizard, but I don't know what sort to get.

Yours faithfully

Tom Bates

Tom Bates

Chalk Cottage

Dear Aunty Jane

Thanks for the book token you sent me. I am going into town with Dad tomorrow and I'm going to buy the new Harry Potter book.

Mum sends her love.

Love from

Nicki

Hi Guys!

Sorry I've been so long in writing to you. It's cool here. There's lots to do. I like the new school. I've got some new friends. I miss you all. Who's in the football team?

See you soon

Lee

Reading

Work with a partner.

1. Complete the activity on **sheet 63**.
2. Imagine you are Chris. Write a letter to a friend, telling them what happened. Make it chatty.

Writing

1. Draft a fan letter to your favourite author.
2. Read it to your partner. Does it sound right? What could you improve?

Extended Writing

Revise your first draft until it is just how you want it.

Make a best copy of the letter and sign it. Then send it to the author.

Don't forget!

- **Explain why you are writing.**
- **Talk about your favourite books.**
- **Ask questions.**

EXTENDED STORY: CHAPTERS

FLOOD! 1

Chapter 1
Marooned!

There had been waterworks on Earlham Road for over a month now!

It took the children a long time to get home. Steve, Jamie and Sam were sick of it.

"I wonder how long this will go on for?" wondered Sam.

Jamie and Steve wondered too.

"It's probably going to take five weeks," said Sam.

The next day the three boys walked to school together. Suddenly they heard a shout from near the roadworks: "HELP!"

They saw water pouring out from the roadworks. So they ran for their lives all the way to school.

They burst through the classroom doors shouting, "FLOOD!"

"Then shut the door!" ordered Charlotte, and so they did.

The Head walked in and said, "I'm sorry children, we are marooned for a month."

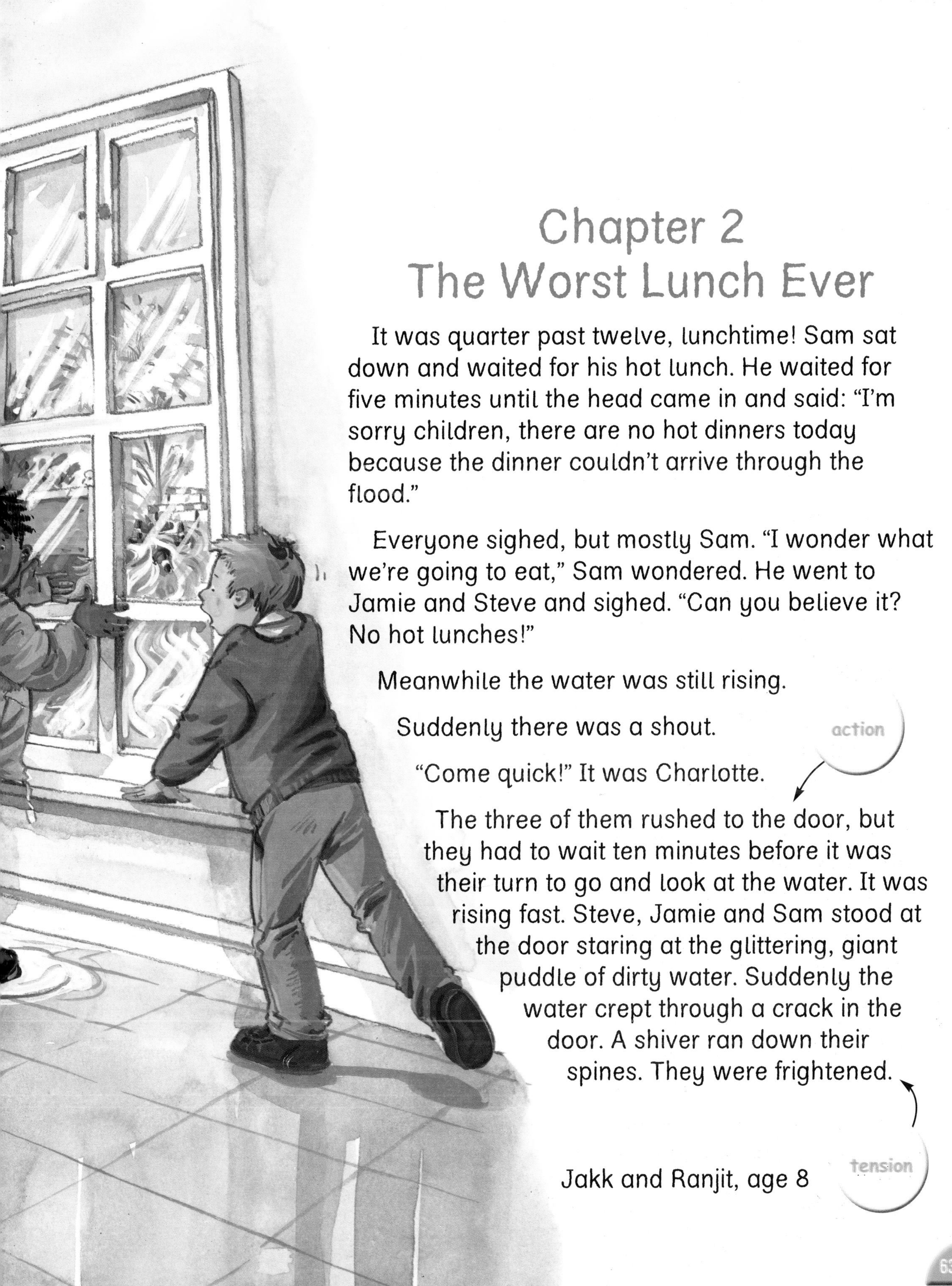

Chapter 2
The Worst Lunch Ever

It was quarter past twelve, lunchtime! Sam sat down and waited for his hot lunch. He waited for five minutes until the head came in and said: "I'm sorry children, there are no hot dinners today because the dinner couldn't arrive through the flood."

Everyone sighed, but mostly Sam. "I wonder what we're going to eat," Sam wondered. He went to Jamie and Steve and sighed. "Can you believe it? No hot lunches!"

Meanwhile the water was still rising.

Suddenly there was a shout.

"Come quick!" It was Charlotte.

The three of them rushed to the door, but they had to wait ten minutes before it was their turn to go and look at the water. It was rising fast. Steve, Jamie and Sam stood at the door staring at the glittering, giant puddle of dirty water. Suddenly the water crept through a crack in the door. A shiver ran down their spines. They were frightened.

Jakk and Ranjit, age 8

action

tension

26 EXTENDED STORY: CHAPTERS

FLOOD! 1

Reading

Work as a group. Use **sheet 65**.

1. What might happen next in the story? How will it end? Use the chapter headings to help you.
2. Make brief notes to say what will happen in each chapter.
3. Write a cliffhanger ending for chapters 3 and 4.

Writing

Work with a partner. Use **sheet 67**.

Plan your own chapter story called '**Trapped**'. Use your homework notes and the ideas from shared writing to help you.

Extended Writing

Finish your story plans. Swap them with another pair and talk about the good and bad points. Revise your plan.

27 EXTENDED STORY: PARAGRAPHS

FLOOD! 2

Look again at the story on pages 62–63.

Reading

Work with a partner.

1. Look at Chapter 2 of '**Flood!**' by Jakk and Ranjit. What bits could they improve? What bits could they take out? What details could they add?

   Make notes on **sheet 68**.

2. Write down some different words for 'sighed', 'wondered' and 'suddenly'.

Writing

Work with a partner on the story you planned.
Draft at least one chapter of the story together.

- paragraphs
- dialogue
- action
- details
- tension

Extended Writing

1. Using your plan, finish drafting the story.
2. Read through and revise the story. Produce a final, illustrated version.

28 ONOMATOPOEIA

The Sound Collector

Morning

Morning comes
 with a milk-float jiggling

Morning comes
 with a milkman whistling

Morning comes
 with empties clinking

Morning comes
 with alarm-clock ringing

Morning comes
 with toaster popping

Morning comes
 with letters dropping

Morning comes
 with kettle singing

Morning comes
 with me just listening

Morning comes to drag me out of bed
 – Boss-Woman Morning

Grace Nichols

Reading

Work as a group and prepare to read aloud three verses of **'The Sound Collector'**. Use **sheet 71**.

1. Read your three verses. Underline the onomatopoeic words. How will you read them? Make notes.
2. Practise reading the poem through.

Writing

PCM 73

Write your own **'Afternoon'** poem.

Think of your own ideas for words and sounds. Use your homework notes and the work from shared writing to help you.

1. Finish writing your **'Afternoon'** poem. Read it through with a partner, and make changes to improve it.
2. Illustrate a final copy of your poem for a class poetry book.

ONOMATOPOEIA:

- use the most interesting sounds
- invent words if you need to

A to Z Book

North American Indians

Animals

Animals were very important to the North American Indians. They used them for food, and to make tipis and clothing. The animals which they used most were buffalo (*see below*), elk, deer, dogs (*see below*) and horses.

Buffalo

The buffalo was the most important animal to the North American Indians. They ate them, and stretched their skins to make tipis. The buffalo's thick furry coat could be made into warm clothes or blankets.

Clothes

The North American Indians made most of their clothes from animal skins. Some tribes made clothes by weaving wool. They made dresses for the girls out of deer skins and thick coats for the men from buffalo skins. They also made shoes called moccasins.

Corn

Corn was an important crop for North American Indians. It was one of the main sources of food, and it was also important in their ceremonies and religions.

Dogs

The North American Indians kept dogs like we do today. They used the dogs to help them hunt, and to pull sledges.

Jade, age 10

Reading

1. Read Jade's report on **sheet 74**.
2. Pick out the key words. Which could you use as headings for an A to Z book? Write them down in alphabetical order.
3. Write a short entry for your first heading.

Writing

Work with a partner.

1. Choose a key word which begins with your letter. This will be the heading for your entry.
2. Draft the entry. Read it through together. Is it clear?
3. Choose another key word and draft another entry.

Extended Writing

Write more entries for your letter of the alphabet. Or ask for another letter.

Don't forget!

- key words as headings
- short entries
- 'see below' or 'above' when an entry is linked to another one

What makes a good writer?

What does a good writer do?

- thinks, concentrates, uses interesting words
- puts in details, uses own life and imagination
- sees it in their head
- makes you want to go on reading
- writes a good ending
- thinks about who it's for

How does someone become a good writer?

- Practising, drafting and revising, reading a lot, going around noticing things, keeping a notebook.

What different kinds of story writing do you do?

- Ghost stories, adventure, traditional tales, animals, football stories.

What writing of yours are you proud of?

- The chapter book I wrote about kids who lived in an orphanage. It took me ages. It looks like a proper book.

What do you find hard?

- Finding the right word, spelling, getting going, the ending.

What do you find easy?

- Working with a partner, brainstorming ideas.

Reading

Work as a group or in pairs.

1. Read the statements on **sheet 75**.
2. Talk about them. Which ones do you agree with? Which do you disagree with? Which don't you know about?
3. Fill in the chart together.

Writing

Work with your partner.

1. Help each other to remember the writing you have done this year.
2. Add blobs to the spider diagram on **sheet 77**.
3. Finish the sentences at the bottom of the sheet.

Extended Writing

Write a short summary of the writing you have done this year. End it with your targets for next year.

Acknowledgements

The publisher would like to thank the following for permission to use their copyright material.

TEXT
Unit 2: extract from *Kamla and Kate* by Jamila Gavin (Egmont Children's Books Ltd) reproduced by permission of David Higham Associates; extract from *Even Stevens F C* by Michael Rosen (HarperCollins) reprinted by permission of HarperCollins Publishers; **Unit 3**: adapted from *Me and My Pet Cat* by Christine Morley and Carol Orbell (Two-Can Publishing Ltd, 1996) reproduced by permission of Two-Can Publishing; **Unit 4**: from *Harry's Party* by Chris Powling, (A&C Black, 1989) reproduced by permission of A&C Black (Publishers) Ltd; **Unit 5**: extract from *Ace Dragon Ltd* by Russell Hoban (Jonathan Cape, 1980) reproduced by permission of David Higham Associates; **Unit 7**: 'Tyrannosaurus Rex' and 'Tunnel' by Stanley Cook, © the estate of Stanley Cook and reproduced by permission of Mrs S Matthews; 'Rhythm Machine' by Trevor Harvey, from *Words Whirl* ed John Foster (OUP, 1998) reproduced by permission of the author; **Unit 9**: extracts from 'Tomato 1' and 'Tomato 2' © Michael Rosen, taken from *The Hypnotiser* (Andre Deutsch Children's Books/Scholastic Children's Books, 1990); 'Battle Lines' by Sandy Brownjohn, from *Word Games* (Hodder and Stoughton), reproduced by permission of the author; **Unit 10**: extract one from *The Strongest Girl in the World* by Sally Gardner (Orion), reproduced by permission of the Orion Publishing Group Ltd; extract two from 'The Pudding Like a Night on the Sea', from *The Julian Stories* © Ann Cameron, 1981 (Victor Gollancz/Hamish Hamilton, 1983) reproduced by permission of Penguin Books Ltd; **Unit 16**: 'Too Much Searching' from *The Crest and the Hide and Other African Stories* by Harold Courlander, (copyright) 1982 Harold Courlander, reproduced by permission of the Emma Courlander Trust; **Unit 17**: 'Mighty Mountain' by Irene Hedlund, from *Stories Round the World*, (A&C Black), reproduced by permission of A&C Black (Publishers) Ltd; **Unit 21**: extracts adapted from *Creatures of the Deep* by Lionel Bender © Aladdin Books, 1989; **Unit 23**: from *Diary of a Killer Cat* © Ann Fine, 1994 (Hamish Hamilton, 1994) reproduced by permission of Penguin Books Ltd; **Unit 28**: 'Morning' by Grace Nichols, from *Give Yourself a Hug* © Grace Nichols, 1994 (A&C Black Ltd, 1994) reproduced by permission of Curtis Brown Ltd, London, on behalf of the author.

ILLUSTRATIONS
Unit 1: Jamila Gavin photograph © Kate Vandyck, 1993; **Unit 2**: artwork for *Kamla and Kate* by Kay Widdowson; artwork for *Even Stevens FC* by Rhian Nest James; **Unit 3**: artwork by Nick Spender; **Unit 4**: artwork by Lisa Williams; **Unit 5**: artwork by Liz Catchpole; **Unit 6**: artwork by Lauren Foster; photos © Simon Warner; **Unit 7**: artwork by Carey Bennet; artwork for *Stanley Cook* Jamie Sneddon; **Unit 8**: page 18, left, P Clement/Bruce Coleman Collection; right, Andrew Purcell/Bruce Coleman Collection; page 19 photo © Martin Sookias; page 20, artwork by Karen Homer; **Unit 9**: artwork by Celia Witchard; **Unit 10**: opening 1, artwork by Melanie Mansfield; opening 2, artwork by Sarah Warburton; opening 3, artwork by Kay Widdowson; **Unit 11**: artwork by Lauren Foster; photographs © Keith Lillis, with thanks to the staff and pupils of Gallions School, London E6; **Unit 12**: artwork by Nick Schon; **Unit 13**: artwork by Lauren Foster; photograph © Chris Honeywell; **Unit 14**: artwork by Martin Ursell; **Unit 15**: artwork by Carla Daly; **Unit 16**: artwork by Jill Newton; **Unit 17**: artwork by Kiran Ahmad; **Unit 18**: artwork by Julian Baker; **Unit 20**: artwork by Barbara Vagnozzi; **Unit 21**: page 51, top, Astrofoto/Bruce Coleman Collection; page 51, bottom and page 52, top, Martin Dohrn/Bruce Coleman Collection; page 52, bottom, Erik Bjurstrom/Bruce Coleman Collection; page 53, top Pacific Stock/Bruce Coleman Collection, bottom Heather Angel; **Unit 23**: artwork by Lizzy Finlay; **Unit 24**: photo © Keith Lillis, with thanks to the staff and pupils of Gallions School, London E6; **Unit 25**; photo © Chris Honeywell; **Unit 26**: artwork by Sheilagh McNicholas; **Unit 28**: artwork by Melanie Mansfield; **Unit 29**: page 68, both photos © Peter Newark's Western Americana; page 69 © Peter Newark's American Pictures; **Unit 30**: photo © Chris Honeywell.

Every effort has been made to trace all copyright holders. The publisher would be glad to hear from any unacknowledged sources at the first opportunity.